Fighting for Gold

Fighting for Gold

Lorna Schultz Nicholson

James Lorimer & Company, Ltd., Publishers
Toronto

James Lorimer & Company Ltd. acknowledges the support of the Canada Council for the Arts and the Ontario Arts Council for our publishing program. We acknowledge the financial support of the Government of Canada through the Book Publishing Industry Development Program (BPIDP) for our publishing activities. We acknowledge the Government of Ontario through the Ontario Media Development Corporation's Ontario Book Initiative.

Cover design by Meghan Collins

Library and Archives Canada Cataloguing in Publication

Schultz Nicholson, Lorna
  Fighting for gold : the story of Canada's sledge hockey Paralympic gold / Lorna Schultz Nicholson.

(Recordbooks)
ISBN 978-1-55277-031-3 (bound).--ISBN 978-1-55277-030-6 (pbk.)

  1. Hockey players with disabilities--Canada--Juvenile literature. 2. Hockey--Juvenile literature. 3. Sports for people with disabilities-- Juvenile literature. 4. Paralympics (9th : 2006 : Turin, Italy)-- Juvenile literature. I. Title. II. Series.

GV848.C29S39 2008   j796.962'08730971   C2008-904677-3

James Lorimer & Company Ltd., Publishers
317 Adelaide Street West,
Suite #1002
Toronto, ON
M5V 1P9
www.lorimer.ca

Distributed in the United States by:
Orca Book Publishers
P.O. Box 468
Custer, WA USA
98240-0468

Printed and bound in Canada

Contents

To all Paralympic athletes. You are an inspiration to everyone because of your dedication, determination, courage and willingness to succeed no matter what the obstacles.

Prologue

Tension filled the arena. Nerves tingled. One by one, the Canadian players pushed their sledges onto the ice. In the stands, the Swedish fans cheered.

Norway and Canada were competing in the semifinal at the 2004 International Paralympic Committee (IPC) World Sledge Hockey Championship in Ornskoldsvik, Sweden. The winning team would go on to the gold-medal game. The loser would play for the bronze medal.

The players just wanted the game to start. Then all the pressure could be put into hard hits, zinging shots, battles in front of the net, and the race to be first to the puck.

Over the years, Canada and Norway had become sledge hockey rivals. Norway had beat Canada in the gold-medal game at the 1998 Paralympics in Nagano, Japan. But then Canada had come back in 2000 to beat Norway, winning the IPC World Sledge Hockey Championship in Salt Lake City. Two years later, Canada had come a dismal fourth at the 2002 Paralympics. To win at the Paralympics put a team on top of the world. To lose, and not take home a medal, seemed like failure.

The Canadian players warmed up by shooting on their goalie, Paul "Rosey" Rosen. Backup goalie Greg Westlake was taking shots too, in case he had to play.

Hervé Lord and Shawn Matheson, veteran players on the Canadian team, knew how important this game was. They had played in every World Championship and Paralympic Games that included sledge hockey. Team captain Todd Nicholson, another veteran, was too sick to play. The entire team missed Todd; he was a good leader. Assistant captain Jean Labonté had been made captain. Now, it was his job to pull the team together. The team had a lot of new young guys. Marc Dorion, Raymond Grassi, Mark Noot, and Benoit St-Amand were all playing in their first World Championship.

The two young high-scorers for Team Canada, Billy Bridges and Bradley Bowden, took their positions at centre ice. The puck dropped. The players battled hard. Their effort showed in their speed on the ice and struggles for the puck. When the buzzer sounded to end the first period, the score was 0–0.

Off the ice, the Canadian players tried to regroup. They talked about game plays. They talked strategy. Sweat dripped off their brows.

When the ice was ready, the players headed out for another period. Bodies crashed against each other along the boards. The game turned vicious. The Canadian players gritted their teeth and shot the puck as hard as they could. They fired off blazing shots. But so did Norway. Shots hit posts, and the ringing sound echoed off the arena walls.

But not one shot went in, for either team. At the end of the second period the score was still 0–0.

The Canadians felt they could win. They could bring gold back to Canada and carry this win into the next Paralympic Games in 2006 in Turin, Italy. Norway was fast, so Canada had to beat their opponents to the puck. They had to hit the Norwegians along the boards, knocking them off the puck. The Canadians had to pass the puck around in the offensive zone. And they had to keep shooting on the net.

The third period started. The players should have been tired from two intense periods of hockey, but they came out flying. They drove their sledge sticks into the ice and propelled their sledges forward. When the play shifted, they twirled around and moved the other way.

At the end of the third period, the score was still 0–0. Not one goal had been scored by either team in three periods of play.

The game went into sudden-death overtime.

For most players, it had been the most gruelling game they had ever played. The Canadians were tired. But they couldn't give up the fight. Their coach, Jeff Snyder, tried to get the team motivated to play and win.

During the overtime period, Canada fought with everything they had. But a Norwegian player rifled off a point shot that sailed into the back of the net. It stopped the Canadians in their tracks. How could they have lost?

There were very few reporters at the game. Sledge hockey wasn't that well-known in Canada, and didn't make front-page news, but the bad news did make it back to Canada.

"Canada will not get a chance to defend its title at the world sledge championship after a 1–0 overtime loss to Norway in the semifinals yesterday," the Canadian Press reported.

The Canadian team was so upset about the loss that they came out flat in their bronze medal game against Sweden. They had no energy left. They didn't take home a medal. They came fourth. The loss stung.

After their fourth place finish the players talked about getting their revenge at the Paralympics in 2006. They all wanted to keep playing, and try out for that team. But the team needed support to get to the Paralympic Games. How could they get people to care about their chances to win gold for Canada? How could they get people in Canada to learn all about the great sport called sledge hockey?

1 A Quick, Hard-hitting Game

Sledge hockey is still a game that not everyone knows a lot about. But because it is exciting and fast-paced, it is becoming a sport that people love to watch.

It all started in 1961 in Stockholm, Sweden, on a frozen lake near a rehab centre. Three wheelchair athletes who had played hockey before becoming disabled wanted to keep playing the game. They invented a new game they played on sleds. The sled they designed had a metal frame

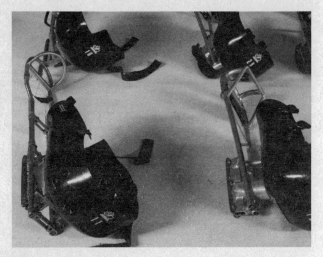

Sledges have regular skate blades on the bottom of them.

that sat on two skate blades. They made sticks out of bike handles.

The three men encouraged others to play, including those who were able-bodied. This helped the sport grow, and by the late 1960s there was a five-team league in Sweden that included both the disabled and the able-bodied.

The new sport quickly spread. The

Winter Games for Disabled Athletes

The Paralympic Games are held every four years in the summer and the winter right after the Olympic Games. The first Winter Paralympic Games were in 1976 and included alpine skiing and nordic skiing. Luge was a demonstration sport. Sixteen countries participated, and there were 250 athletes in total. The Winter Paralympic Games quickly grew to include Ice Sledge Hockey in 1998 and Wheelchair Curling in 2006.

Swedish players showed sledge hockey to the Norwegians. Norway showed sledge hockey to Great Britain. In 1981 Canada started playing sledge hockey. Ten years later they put together an international team. In 1991 the first World Cup sledge tournament was held. Canada won gold!

In 1994 sledge hockey was a demonstration sport at the Paralympic

This is the front of a sledge.

Winter Games in Lillehammer, Norway. Often new sports are included as demonstration sports first to see if they should become full medal sports in later Games. Canada, Norway, Estonia, Sweden, and Great Britain participated. Canada won a bronze medal. Sledge hockey was so well-received that it became a full medal sport at the 1998 Paralympics in Nagano, Japan.

At the international level, sledge hockey

Ray Grassi (#21) likes to use a bucket sledge.

is played by men with lower body
disabilities. Just like in able-bodied hockey,
each team has six players on the ice: one
goalie, two defence, and three forwards.

A hockey sledge is made up of a plastic
seat attached to a metal frame. This frame
sits on two regular-sized skate blades, high
enough that the puck can pass
underneath. Every player has a sledge that

Graeme Murray (#29) goes after a loose puck.

is custom-made to fit the player's body and disability. The athlete is strapped in the sledge at the ankles, knees, and hips. All sledge players must wear protective gear, including a full face mask.

Players carry two sticks, both only 75 cm (29.5 inches) long. They are about the size of a mini-stick. But unlike plastic mini-sticks, sledge hockey sticks are made of durable metal or wood. Each curved stick has a razor-sharp pick on one end and a hockey-stick blade on the other end. The players dig the pick end of the sticks into the ice to push the sledge forward. The picks also help the players stop and turn. The curved blade of the stick is used to stick-handle the puck.

Sledge hockey sticks have picks on the bottom.

Sliding their hands up and down their sticks lets sledge players use both ends. They only shoot with one hand at a time but they can shoot with both left and right hands. This is very hard to do. But the Canadian sledge players make it look easy. They have great stick-handling skills, and can pass the puck under the sledge and over to a teammate while the sledge is moving. And when they shoot the puck, they shoot it hard.

Sledge players are so low to the ground that they can't use the hockey benches in most arenas. They certainly can't jump over the boards. The players' box is usually on the ice so the players can make the quick line changes needed to play fast-paced hockey. Some arenas holding sledge events have made the boards by the players' bench out of Plexiglas. They are level with the ice surface so sledge players can go behind the bench.

Body-checking is allowed in sledge hockey. For a sledge player, hitting the boards is like hitting cement. Players often end up with bruises when the game is over. And sometimes, when a player hits another player, they both fall over. But they bounce right back up.

Sledge hockey has the same penalties as able-bodied hockey. But there is one extra

Important Dates in Sledge Hockey

1961, Sweden: A club team tries sledge hockey on a lake.

1967, Sweden: Sledge hockey is played on a regular outdoor rink.

1969: Norway gets a sledge team.

1981: Great Britain gets a sledge team.

1981: Canada starts a sledge team.

1988: The USA starts a sledge team.

2006: Sledge hockey is played by athletes in 12 countries.

penalty: T-boning. This is called when a player drives his sledge into another player's sledge at a 90° angle.

Sledge games are made up of three 15-minute periods instead of able-bodied hockey's three 20-minute periods.

Although there are differences between able-bodied hockey and sledge hockey, there is one thing that is the same. It is hockey! Playing in the Paralympics is just as exciting and tough as playing in the Olympics. Hockey Canada says, "No matter how you SAY it, no matter how you PLAY it, it's HOCKEY!"

2 Making the Cut

Months after their hard loss to Norway at the 2004 Worlds, the Canadian sledge hockey team heard some good news about their sport. Hockey Canada was going to vote to include the sledge hockey team under their umbrella. Hockey Canada takes care of Minor hockey, the World Junior teams, the Senior World Championship teams, the Women's National teams, and the coveted Men's and Women's Olympic teams. Being part of Hockey Canada instead of Sledge Hockey of Canada (SHOC), sledge players would get funding for their trips and new equipment. Hockey Canada would apply for grants. One would be to hire a full-time person to run the sport and the other to get federal government funding. This might mean the sledge athletes would actually receive money, just like other Canadian athletes. Plus, more importantly, their sport would become more well-known.

In May 2004, at the Hockey Canada annual general meeting, the members of the Hockey Canada board took the vote. And they voted to have the Canadian Sledge Hockey Team as a part of Hockey Canada.

When the sledge players heard the news, they were excited. They knew what a difference the support of Hockey Canada would make. Rosey Rosen phoned Jean Labonté at his home in Montreal right

Billy Bridges (#18) taking a faceoff against a Norwegian player.

away. Jean couldn't believe it.

"When we come to events there are high expectations," said Jean to the Paralympic News Service. "Those expectations were there before, but now they are a little different. It's true we have to perform but we want to show we are worthy of the funding."

With the boost from Hockey Canada

the players felt they could win the gold medal at the 2006 Paralympics in Turin, Italy. What they needed was a coach. And now Hockey Canada was in charge of hiring the coach for the team.

Jeff Snyder really wanted to keep his job as coach of the sledge hockey team. He had started out coaching able-bodied hockey. In 2002, less than two years after he had quit coaching a Major Junior team in Kitchener, Jeff had received a phone call. At that time Jeff knew little about sledge hockey. "I got a call from out of the blue," he later said in an interview for the official Paralympics website, "wondering if I was interested in coaching Canada's National Sledge Hockey team. I didn't really know what the sport was all about and wasn't sure if I wanted to do it or not."

When Jeff showed up at that first sledge practice he had no idea what to expect. The dressing room was filled with wheelchairs and artificial legs. At the gate to the ice surface, the men strapped themselves into their sledges. They pushed their sledges onto the ice, and started playing.

Jeff had never seen anything like it before. The players moved incredibly fast in their sledges. They passed the puck with total accuracy. They fired off hard, fast shots with just one hand. They could go one way in their sledges then spin around and head in the other direction almost instantly.

Jeff learned about the men and their lives. They had overcome so much yet they played their sport with passion, skill, and dedication.

Jeff's respect for the players started right away. After that first practice, he even decided to get into a sledge just to see what it was like. Trying it out with his daughter, he soon saw that it wasn't easy. "The hardest part was just keeping our balance. We really discovered that sledge hockey players have to do everything at once, including pushing with their picks and puck handling. My hat is off to these guys with incredible agility."

On April 21, 2005, Jeff was excited to be named head coach for Canada's National Sledge Hockey team. He was taking Canada to the 2006 Paralympics in

Hockey By Any Other Name

Sledge hockey is a sport that is played across Canada. Many cities are trying to make sledge hockey available to as many players as possible. The London Blizzard Organization has male and female players ages seven and up. Some other teams from across Canada include: the Edmonton Sledge Dogs; Hamilton Sledgehammers; London Blizzard; Sudbury Northern Sliders; North Bay Icebreakers; Estevan, Saskatchewan Assoc-iation; Durham Steelhawks; BC Eagle Sledge; and the Windsor Ice Bullets.

Turin, Italy! He would have the job of picking 24 players to be invited to a selection camp on June 10–12 in Ottawa, Ontario. After that, he had until February 2006 to name his team.

Jeff was curious to see how his veterans would make out. Hervé Lord, Todd Nicholson, and Shawn Matheson had played in every Paralympics up until then: 1994, 1998, and 2002. And they had never won a gold medal. Could they make the 2006 team? Or were they too old?

With pen and paper, Jeff sat in the stands and watched Hervé Lord as he cruised to centre ice to take the faceoff. Hervé won the faceoff, sending the puck to his winger. Then he went wide. Hervé Lord was 48 years old, the oldest guy on the team. With power, he pushed his sledge forward, looking for a pass. He was still in great physical shape. The pass went to a player on the other team. With pure grit

Hervé sailed over and hit the player as hard as he could. Hervé was a leader and a hard hitter, good defensively and good at faceoffs. Jeff felt he deserved a spot on the team.

Next out was Todd. He moved around the ice, constantly watching the puck and the other team. Todd knew exactly where to go when he was on the ice. He saw the puck coming to him, looked up the ice, saw his linemate, and rifled off a pass. Then he sailed forward. Once at the net, Todd circled, getting open. When the shot hit the net, he was right there for the rebound. It was clear that Todd would be a good player to put between two young guys. His experience would help in key games. But could he stay healthy enough to play?

The third veteran on the team was Shawn Matheson. Shawn moved to the net, but his speed just wasn't quite there.

There were younger players who were skilled and fast. Jeff wasn't sure about Shawn.

When the camp was over, Jeff had to name 17 players who would attend the four scheduled training camps. In the end, only 15 of those players would make the final roster. Number 17 on the list was Shawn. He had squeaked by because of his experience.

Shawn called Jeff and asked what he had to do to make the team. Jeff said that Shawn would have to become more of a hitter. Shawn had been known as a goal-scorer, but now he would have to change gears. There were young players who were skilled with the puck. Jeff knew that Shawn had gotten a taste of being a star player and that changing roles was hard for some older players.

At the final selection camp in January, Shawn pushed onto the ice to take his shift. A winger moved down the boards. Shawn chased him. When he was close enough, he squared his shoulder and laid a hard, clean hit. All through the training camp, Shawn had done everything Jeff had told him to do.

The final roster was announced at a press conference on February 27, 2006. All three veteran players had made the cut, with Todd being named captain. Most of the players had been to the Paralympics before: Jeremy Booker, Bradley Bowden, Billy Bridges, Jean Labonté, Graeme Murray, Rosey Rosen, Dany Verner. Benoit St-Amand, who had played forward for the World Championship team in 2004, was going to be backup goalie. Greg Westlake was playing out instead of in net. Marc Dorion, Raymond Grassi, and Mark Noot had played for the 2004 World team, but had never played in the Paralympics.

After the final roster was announced, President of Hockey Canada, Bob Nicholson, got up to speak. He said, "On behalf of Hockey Canada, I'd like to extend my best wishes to all the members of Canada's Sledge Team. Their devotion and commitment to this very challenging and exciting sport is fantastic, and I look forward to watching them in Turin."

At the close of the press conference Jeff stepped up to the microphone. "The players and staff have been working very hard to prepare to represent Canada successfully at the Paralympics in Turin. We are looking forward to a great competition and feel that we are ready to challenge for the gold medal."

The 15 players, the management, and coaching staff were leaving for Turin five days after the team announcement.

3 Getting to Turin

On March 4, 2006, coach Jeff Snyder stood in the Montreal airport, passport in hand. His team was ready to head for Italy.

Team captain Todd Nicholson wheeled his chair through the airport. Todd was an experienced traveller, so he was four hours early. He had to be. He was in a wheelchair, and getting on and off the airplane took extra time.

Todd hadn't always been in a wheelchair. When he was young he had played able-bodied hockey, soccer, and basketball. On the way home from his high-school prom, he had driven his car into a tree stump and ended up in a hospital for more than a year. The doctors told him he'd never walk again. When he finally got out of the hospital, his life was different. But Todd didn't want to give up sports. He found out about sledge hockey, and right away he started playing and working hard at this new sport. Over the years he had trained as hard as any Olympic athlete because his goal had been to go to the Paralympics. Now here he was, going to his fourth Paralympics.

Boarding a plane was always a challenge for Todd and the other players in wheelchairs. Most of them had to be piggy-backed onto the plane and to their seats. The guys with artificial legs had it a little easier because they could walk to their seats.

Turin or Bust

Between selection camp in June 2005 and leaving for Turin, Todd Nicholson had been fighting just to stay healthy. His problems started on a golf course in late August 2005. After playing 13 holes, Todd found he couldn't push his chair. He found he had an infected sore on his hip bone. Even after surgery, the infection wouldn't go away. Over the next couple of months Todd had six surgeries and rested in bed until December 1. Sick or not, Todd was going to Italy. His doctor showed him how to bandage his wound using a mirror to see what he was doing.

Rosey walked on the plane and sat down. At 46 years old, he was older than all of his teammates except for Hervé. When he was just a teenager, Rosey was playing able-bodied hockey and had caught his foot in a rut. He had broken his leg in 14 places. The leg had healed, but then he had broken it again. Doctors had performed 23 surgeries trying to fix the damage. On surgery number 24 they had amputated his leg just above the knee.

Rosey leaned back in his seat and thought about the 12-year-old boy who had told him about a sport he could play. The kid had told Rosey that sledge hockey looked cool, and that he should give it a try. Rosey had gone to a game, cruising onto the ice in a borrowed sledge. The players had whizzed by him. Rosey knew he wanted to play this game but he could see he wasn't fast enough. Right then he had decided that, since he had liked to play catcher in baseball, maybe he could try being a sledge goalie.

The game gave Rosey a challenge. He knew his three children were proud of him. He had played in the Paralympic Games in 2002, and now he was headed to Turin for his second Paralympics.

Hervé Lord took off his prosthetic leg for long flights. If his leg started to swell, the plastic from the artificial leg could dig into his skin.

Hervé had been in a horrible car accident near Calgary, Alberta, when he was 28 years old. He'd spent over a year in hospital. After 11 surgeries they had amputated his leg just above his knee. His accident, the result of driving too fast, made him see that he had been given a second chance to do something with his life.

Hervé usually sat beside his good friend Jean Labonté on long flights. Jean had been named the assistant captain of the team and was a great sledge player.

When Jean was 17, he found out he had a tumour on his left tibia, a bone in the lower leg. He had lost his leg to the cancer when he was 20 years old. Five years after losing his leg, Jean started playing sledge hockey. Urging on his young friend, Hervé had told Jean, "Hockey is hockey."

After speaking a few words in French to each other, Hervé and Jean leaned back and tried to sleep during the long flight overseas.

The plane bumped, and landed on the Paris runway. The team had a stopover in Paris before flying the rest of the way to Turin.

For Shawn the travelling never got any easier. The stump on his right leg swelled. It gave him a dull, achy pain that started in the stump and moved to his backside and lower back. As he strapped on his prosthetic leg, it cut into his skin. Without saying one word about the pain, Shawn stood up, grabbed his bag and headed off the plane.

When Shawn Matheson was 16 years old he had lost his right leg, just above the knee, to cancer. In the hospital he had decided that he couldn't dwell on what he had lost. As soon as his leg healed, he immediately got involved in sledge hockey and in wheelchair track and field.

Landing in Paris, the players found out that their own wheelchairs were still in storage. They were told they would have to use other, much smaller wheelchairs.

Todd was angry and wanted his chair. Marc Dorion agreed with Todd, but he let the older players handle the situation.

This was Marc's first Paralympics and he was just 18 years old. The 2004 World Championships had been his first time playing international sport. But he'd been playing sledge hockey since he was four years old. Marc had been in a wheelchair all his life because he had been born with spina bifida. To not have his own wheelchair was like not having a part of his body.

Like Marc, Jeremy Booker was born

with spina bifida and had been in a chair since he was young. He had played in the 2002 Paralympics in Salt Lake City at the age of 16 — the youngest player on the team. Now there was no way he wanted someone pushing him in some small wheelchair.

Also piping up was Billy Bridges. Billy had been born with a spinal cord disability. All his life, he'd watched hockey and dreamed he could play in the NHL. Ever since he had started playing sledge hockey when he was 12, he had faced problems that a pro player would never imagine.

In the Paris airport, tempers flared. Todd refused to go through customs without his own chair. Bradley Bowden, Mark Noot, and Dany Verner also said they wanted their own wheelchairs. Graeme Murray wanted to use his own chair, but waited quietly.

Graeme had been paraplegic since he

was three years old. He'd had a severe asthma attack. While he was in the hospital, a rare virus had attacked the nerves in his lower spine.

It was unfair that the players could not use their own wheelchairs. And it was not only the "wheelies," or players in wheelchairs, who felt that way. Greg Westlake added his voice to the issue.

Greg was also one of the young guys, just short of his 22nd birthday. As an "amp," or amputee, Greg felt lucky to be one of the guys who could walk. His feet had been amputated when he was just 18 months old. For as long as he could remember he'd had artificial feet. All his life he'd played able-bodied sports, and hockey had been his favourite. He had switched to sledge hockey and made the National Sledge team in 2003. "At first it felt weird to be playing on a team with people in wheelchairs," Greg had said.

The Making of a Team

A sledge hockey team is often made up of players with different disabilities. Instead of the usual sledge, some players who have both legs amputated above the knee use a shorter enclosed sledge called a bucket sledge. Off the ice, some use wheelchairs to get around, and some can walk on their own or with the help of things like canes or crutches. On the Canadian team, there was good-natured teasing between the players in wheelchairs — the "wheelies" — and the amputees, or "amps."

"But I'm playing at the highest possible level somebody with a disability can play. I'm playing for Team Canada representing my country. Though the dream isn't exactly how I envisioned it, I think I'm a better person today than if I never played sledge hockey. I couldn't be happier with how my life is right now."

Like Greg, Benoit St-Amand and Ray

Grassi were not part of the wheelchair group, but they just kept quiet.

Todd's complaining paid off. The athletes got their own wheelchairs. After the wheelies were in their chairs, Hockey Canada personnel broke the bad news. The team couldn't all go on the same flight. The smaller planes couldn't take that many passengers in wheelchairs.

The team would have to split up.

4 Coming Together as a Team

All the Paralympic athletes were housed at the Olympic Village in Turin. Arriving at the Olympic Village, the players found a group of small colourful houses. Five or six players would share a house. Each house had one or two bedrooms on the main floor and another two bedrooms upstairs. This meant some guys would have to take an elevator. And the elevators were small. They would only fit one wheelchair, maybe two.

After unpacking, the players were given a tour. They liked the big common area where they could all hang out. In the village there was a cafeteria and an arcade room. The all-you-can-eat food service made everyone happy. So did the free sports drinks.

The Canadian players and coaching staff wondered what the arena would be like. They had some ice time that night, but only half the players would be at practice because of the flight changes. When Jeff arrived at the arena he saw that the organizers had put Plexiglas in the hallways. This was not a good thing. It would dull the sledge blades. They would have to think of another way to get the players to the ice.

At the arena the next day, Dany Verner looked at the acrylic lining the hallway. Dany had arrived on the later flight, so this was his first visit to the arena. He decided that he would crawl to the ice so he wouldn't dull his sledge blades. Dany had been born with spina bifida and had started playing sledge hockey at the age of 11. He'd played for Canada at two other Paralympic Games. But each one had its own challenges.

In some arenas, the team got a trolley that would transport them to the ice. Over the years they had nicknamed the trolley the "amp mobile."

Raymond Grassi had another idea about how to get to the ice surface. At 188 cm (6 feet 2 inches) and 104 kg (230 pounds), Ray wore the nickname "Big Guy" proudly. When he was born they had to amputate both of his legs. He had just started playing sledge hockey three years before. Hitting was his specialty.

One by one the players left the room. When it was Ray's turn, he yanked a skateboard out of his hockey bag. He balanced himself on the skateboard and, using his arms, wheeled down the hall. When he got to the end of the hall there was a ramp. How was he going to get up the ramp and onto the ice? Ray noticed a few Italian arena staff members milling around. He called them over and asked if they would give him a push.

They got behind Ray's skateboard. On the count of a one-two-three, in Italian, they pushed Ray up the ramp.

At the ice, the players strapped themselves into their sledges. Each sledge was custom-fitted and precious to its player. All the players liked to fit tight in their sledges. Any extra movement in the sledge could cause blisters. It could also slow a player down. Many players brought two identical sledges so they could have one for backup.

Using his arms to lift himself, Mark Noot plunked his body in his bucket sledge. Only a few guys on the team used a bucket sledge. Most used sledges that were long and open. Mark wiggled his body down until he felt snug and tight.

Mark had lost both his legs, just above his knees, to meningitis when he was 22 years old. When he first lost his legs, he wondered about his life. What could he do? He could still fish. And his love for cars wouldn't change either. A true Canadian, Mark had always enjoyed watching hockey games, and Wayne Gretzky was his favourite player. So one day, he'd tried sledge hockey. Mark played for six years with the Kitchener Sidewinders sledge team and three years on the National Team. This was his first Paralympics.

Goalie Rosey tucked his good leg up under the stump of his amputated leg. Most sledge goalies didn't sit that way, but that's what worked for Rosey. Rosey thought real hockey goalie pads were too bulky, so he wore different equipment. He wore a shin pad on his lower leg. Across his thigh he strapped on a lacrosse kidney pad. He knew he got more bruises that way, but he could move around better. Once he had adjusted his big neck guard, he slid his sledge onto the ice and moved toward his net.

At the net, he twirled his sledge around so he was facing his teammates. The guys lined up to shoot on him. In warm-up, Rosey stopped shot after shot.

Coach Jeff blew his whistle and instructed his players to do the break-out drill. The forwards lined up at one end and the defence at the other. Rosey went in one net and backup goalie Benoit St-Amand went in the other net.

Billy Bridges picked up a loose puck. He dug in his picks and pushed his sledge forward with one stick. With his other hand he stick-handled. Greg and Bradley moved beside him.

Jeff watched Billy. The kid was talented. He had great hands and was good at moving the puck. He could shoot it quickly and pass it dead-on. Billy passed the puck to Greg. Greg passed to Bradley. Jeff knew the three young kids could play against any line from any team. It was great to have Greg playing forward instead of net. They looked focused. Jeff needed them to be good, as they were his goal scorers.

Next up was Todd's line. He was playing with Marc Dorion and Jeremy Booker. Marc and Jeremy were new and young, but were good, solid players. Todd added experience to the line. They flew down the ice, passing and weaving.

The other forwards rounding out the list were Hervé, Shawn, and Dany. Shawn was doing his job. When he got in deep, he crushed one of the defence. Hervé

Jeremy Booker (#8) racing for the puck.

swooped in and took a shot on net. Shawn
was hitting just as Jeff had told him to do.
Back on defence, Ray was solid, as were
Graeme, Mark Noot, and Jean. Todd liked
the defence combinations of Ray with
Mark and Graeme with Jean.

By the end of practice, Jeff relaxed a bit.
The team looked focused and ready to
play. The Paralympic Opening Ceremonies

were on March 10. Then the Games
would begin.

5 Opening Honours

Dressed in their Canadian Paralympic outfits, the team met in the common area of the Olympic Village to head to the Opening Ceremonies.

Jeff noticed that Rosey had running shoes on.

All the Canadian athletes, from all the sports, had been given special boots to match their outfits. Jeff told Rosey to go get his boots.

Rosey pointed to Mark Noot, who was

in his wheelchair. "Noot doesn't have to wear them," he said.

Jeff quickly replied, "Rosey, Noot doesn't have legs. Go get your boots."

Scott Salmond, one of the Hockey Canada managers, watched Rosey head back to his room. Scott tried not to laugh. This was his first trip with the sledge team. Usually he travelled with the World Junior Hockey team or the Men's World Hockey team. He had never seen a team that acted as much like siblings as these players did. They really understood each other and had a special bond. Scott knew that

A Demonstration Sport

At the 1994 Paralympic Games in Norway, sledge hockey was a demonstration sport. This means that the medals won in the event didn't count toward a team's medal count. Canada, Norway, Estonia, Sweden, and Great Britain participated.

Hockey Canada was lucky to have this team under its wing.

Hockey Canada was also proud that Todd Nicholson had been chosen as Canada's flag bearer. Todd would lead the 33 Canadian Paralympic athletes competing in Turin. "It's time to carry Canadian Paralympics Sports to a new level," Todd had said in a Hockey Canada news release, "I know this team is ready to show the world what Canada can do."

The Canadian Paralympics Committee President, Henry Wohler, had said, "Todd is the kind of player who leads by example. He sets a standard for courage and dedication to which we can aspire. He's also one heck of a hockey player!"

Todd's teammates agreed. In the Hockey Canada news release Jean Labonté is quoted: "Selecting Todd is a boost for the whole team, Hockey, Alpine, Nordic, and Curling. He is the man; recognized by all!"

At the Opening Ceremonies, Todd led the Canadian contingent into the stadium with the red-and-white Canadian flag tucked securely into his wheelchair. The sledge hockey players followed him with great pride, as did all the other Canadian Paralympic athletes. Their showy entrance was matched by rest of the Ceremonies, an event coloured with bright fireworks and fantastic entertainment.

At the end of the evening, Jeff called a team meeting back at the Village. He wanted a short session to get the players focused on their first game. They would play the next morning at 9:30 against Great Britain.

When all the players were gathered, Jeff looked around the room. The sledge players were different from any other athletes he had coached. They had such strength, but at the same time were thankful for everything they were given.

In that spirit, Jeff had decided that he wanted everyone to dedicate their Paralympics to someone.

One by one the players made their dedications. They chose mothers, brothers, fathers, and friends who had been there for them during trying times. Then it was Jeff's turn. The players wanted him to pick too. Jeff picked his nephew, Dan Snyder. Dan had been an NHL hockey player, and had died in a car accident.

Todd suggested that the team wear Dan's number on their jerseys. They would all get pins with number 37 on them and wear them through the Games.

Jeff was deeply touched and honoured to be coaching such a great group of athletes.

6 First Game

On the morning of Canada's first sledge hockey game of the Turin Paralympics, the bus pulled up in front of the rink well before game time. Backup goalie Benoit St-Amand headed to the dressing room with his big hockey bag full of goalie equipment. Benoit wouldn't be playing in the game against Great Britain. He walked beside Dany Verner, who was in his wheelchair. They spoke French. Benoit liked that the team included many

French-speaking players on the team.

Benoit had Dany to thank for urging him to play sledge hockey. Benoit had played able-bodied hockey until he had lost his leg to bone cancer at the age of 27. When Benoit had first found out he had cancer, he had been so sick that he couldn't think about getting back on the ice. He had fought the cancer for two years when the doctors told him they would have to amputate his right leg. A few years later Dany had suggested Benoit come and play sledge hockey. As the backup goalie, Benoit wasn't going to play a lot. But that was okay. He just liked being part of the team.

Benoit wore number 22, his number when he had last played able-bodied hockey. Cheering on number 22 were Benoit's parents, who had made the trip to Italy. They were his biggest fans. When he was little, they had always watched his games.

Just before game time, Jeff came in the dressing room to give his pre-game talk. The Canadians knew they were a better team than Great Britain. Jeff told them they still had to play the Canadian tough, skilled hockey game. Because the number of goals counted in the standings, they could have no sympathy. They had to rack up the points.

The crowd roared when the Canadian team flew onto the ice. The Italians had

Canada's sledge hockey team in a huddle before the game.

managed to fill the stands with school-aged children. The children were cheering for the Canadians. Jeff couldn't believe that so many people had come to watch the game.

The puck dropped. Bradley picked it up and sent it flying over to his winger. He dug in his pick and sailed his sledge down the ice. Canada carried the puck into Great Britain's end zone. Fore-checking like crazy, Canada kept the puck in Great Britain's end. After about just a minute of play, Britain took a charging penalty.

Bradley went off for a line change. He skated to the boards and waved his stick in the air. Bradley had been in a chair all his life because he'd been born with problems in his lower back and pelvis. After playing sledge hockey for eight years, he'd made the National Team at 16. Even though he'd made the team for the 2002 Paralympics, he couldn't play because he had a horrible thumb injury. So, this was

Bradley's first Paralympics and he wanted to score some goals.

During the power play, Canada kept shooting. But no one could get the puck in the net. Great Britain's goalie made save after save.

When Canada's power play was over, the puck made it out past centre ice and into Canada's end. The Canadian defence sent the puck right back up the ice and back into Great Britain's end.

Billy took a pass from Greg and cruised over the blue line. He fired a bullet shot. The puck sank to the back of Great Britain's net.

Billy threw his arms in the air. His mother and grandmother cheered from the stands. Canada was on the scoreboard.

Next shift out, Billy ended up in the penalty box for elbowing. Fighting like mad to keep Great Britain from scoring on their power play, Jeremy somehow stole the puck off the fore-check. He spun in front of the net, sliding the puck underneath the goalie and over the line. He scored short-handed to give Canada a 2–0 lead.

Canada kept the pressure on. At the very end of the first period, Bradley saw that Billy was circling in front of the net and fired off a pass to him. Billy took a quick shot. It was just too hard for Great Britain's goalie to handle. Billy had scored his second goal. The first period ended with Canada up 3–0.

The second period started out much like the first. Great fore-checking created a turnover. Bradley came from behind the net to skim the puck in on the goal-side of the post.

With all the goals coming from the young blood, Hervé Lord decided it was time for the old guys to score. He fired off a quick shot from the top of the circle,

Canada's goalie, Paul Rosen (#57), making a great save.

scoring Canada's fifth goal.

On fire, Bradley scored two more goals in the second period. The period ended with Canada ahead 7–0.

In the third period, Bradley added a fourth goal. Billy scored twice more to get a hat trick. In total, the two young players had scored seven of Canada's nine goals. Canada won their opening game 9–0.

7 Hometown Crowd

The buzz that the Canadians had an amazing sledge team raced around the Italian city of Turin. The Canadian team's second game was against the home team Italians on Sunday, March 12, at 5:00 p.m. Tickets sold quickly.

Sunday afternoon, when the Canadians took to the ice, the fans cheered. But then the Italians hit the ice and the noise boomed through the arena.

Billy had never played in front of that

many people before. The excitement of the European crowd would have made anyone nervous.

From his position behind the bench, Jeff could see that there wasn't an empty seat left in the arena. All over the building, the Italians waved their green-and-white flags. Only a few red-and-white flags showed where Canada's fans were sitting.

The crowd cheered through the entire warm-up. When the buzzer sounded to end the warm-up, Jeff brought his team together at the bench. As he addressed his players, he had to yell to be heard.

When the puck dropped the Italians, sparked by their fans, started off with fury. But their speed off the faceoff lasted for only a minute. Todd got the puck on the end of his stick and went flying toward the Italian goal. He had his sledge moving so fast that he ended up sliding over the goal line along with the puck. He raised his arms in triumph. But then the referee signalled *no goal*. Todd had been in the crease when the puck passed the line.

About a minute later, on a pass from Jeremy, Todd got his revenge. He scored on the short side against the Italian goalie.

The cheering of the Italian fans was not enough to keep their country in the game. Just 41 seconds later, Dany sailed across the blue line and lasered the puck past the Italian goalie.

The Canadians peppered the Italian goalie with shots. On defence, Big Ray blasted a shot from the point. Circling the front of the net, Dany managed to tip in the puck, scoring his second of the game.

Just seconds later Graeme took an interference penalty. The Italians were on the power play. Their fans screamed. Marc and Jeremy were put out on the penalty kill. Short-handed, Marc fired a shot, but it rang off the post. The period ended with the Canadians up 3–0.

During the break, Jeff pulled aside Benoit and told him he was putting him in net.

Benoit had flown overseas thinking he might not see any ice at all. But Jeff was letting him replace Rosey in goal. Benoit couldn't wait to get out in front of the sold-out crowd. But more important, he wanted to play for his parents.

The second period started off with a bang. Billy managed to beat the Italian defence to a free puck. He popped it in the net on a high corner shot. After only 11 seconds, the puck was again in the back of the Italian net. Graeme added a fifth Canadian goal a couple of minutes later by moving in on the Italian goalie and sliding it underneath his sledge.

The score remained 5–0 until the last minute of the second period. Billy sank two goals in just eleven seconds, giving him a hat trick.

During the break, Jeff once again told his team that they should try to get as many goals as possible. Norway had already played their second game. To beat them in total goals, Canada needed ten goals in this game. That meant they needed at least three more in the last period. If Canada and Norway ended up winning the same number of games at the end of the round robin, the goal total would make a difference. The more goals they scored the better.

Benoit hoped his team could continue to play well. He wanted the win as goalie. What if he could get a shutout? Benoit blocked that from his mind. It was bad luck to even think the word "shutout" before the end of the game.

Canada came back on the ice ready to play the third period. They kept pressing the Italians. Two minutes into the period,

How a Tournament Works

There were two groups of teams in the 2006 Paralympic sledge hockey tournament. Canada was in Group A with Great Britain, Italy, and their rival team, Norway. They would play a game against each of those teams in the round robin for a total of three games. The four teams in Group B were: United States, Japan, Sweden, and Germany. A win would give a team two points, a tie one point, and a loss no points. For the semi-finals, the first place team in Group A would play the second place team in Group B and vice versa. If there was a tie in the group then the team with the most goals would win. The winners from each of the semi-final games go on to play in the gold medal game. The losers go on to play in the bronze medal game.

Billy got a beautiful pass from Graeme and fired it past the goalie. Then Greg handled a pass from Billy and flipped it in. They really were racking up the score.

At the other end of the rink, Benoit wasn't having to deal with a lot of shots. But getting shots keeps a goalie in the game. Benoit had to keep moving his sledge from side to side to keep his blood flowing. When the play did move into his end, he focused and he stopped every shot.

Canada scored their tenth goal 5:07 into the period. It was an unassisted goal by Graeme, his second goal of the game.

The score remained 10–0 until the last minute of play. Billy put another in. The last and final goal for Canada came with just 17 seconds left in the game. Jean put one past the Italian goalie on a pass from his good friend Hervé.

The score ended 12–0 for the Canadians. Benoit lifted up his goalie mask. His first game in the Paralympics and he had a shutout!

With the win, Canada was guaranteed a spot in the semifinals.

Reporters crowded around to talk to Billy when he left the dressing room. He was Canada's top scorer of the game, with five goals and one assist. When asked what he felt about the game, he said, "We have nothing but respect for the Italian team and we didn't want to embarrass them in front of their fans but we needed to play hard. We really needed to get 10 goals to make first place in case there was a tie-breaker."

After the Canada-Italy game, Billy Bridges had 11 points in the tournament on eight goals and three assists. He was the tournament leading scorer at that point.

Although they had a solid victory over the Italians, the Canadians knew their next game would not be easy.

They had to play Norway.

8 Canada vs. Norway

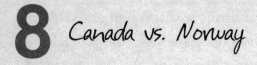

Hockey is a sport that holds famous rivalries. Some teams seem fated to meet again and again in games with a lot at stake. In sledge hockey, Canada's biggest rival was Norway.

When the puck dropped, the pace began. And it was fast. Dressed in their red-white-and-blue jerseys, Norway came out flying.

Star player Rolf Pedersen was playing solid and tough on defence. And their veteran goalie, Roger Johansen, was playing his angles well.

Again, there was a packed arena. Many were cheering for Canada. But many were flying the Norwegian flag.

The puck was in play for only 47 seconds before Norway took a penalty for boarding. Canada went to the power play. High-scoring Billy tried as hard as he could, but he couldn't get the puck in the net. Playing smart hockey, Norway didn't

Rolf Pedersen

Rolf Pedersen is one of Norway's top players. He hits hard but is also very skilled. Rolf is a true competitor and in tournaments he is often racing with Canada's Billy Bridges for the scoring title. In 2008 in Charlottetown, PEI, at the World Sledge Hockey tournament, Rolf scored four goals and also picked up two assists in just one game. Norway beat Japan 8–0, and Rolf was involved in six of the goals.

give the Canadians many good scoring chances.

Then Norway took another penalty for holding. Pedersen went to the penalty box. But even with the two-man advantage for 35 seconds, the Canadians couldn't get the puck past Johansen.

When the teams were back at full strength, Norway cranked up the speed.

Ray Grassi (#21) body-checking a Norwegian player.

They fought against the Canadians. The Canadians fought back. But then Norway took a pass out front to slide the puck under Rosey's sledge. It cruised to the back of the net and Norway was up 1–0.

Canada regrouped. They couldn't let themselves get down. All they could think of was hitting. Every shift, they went out and tried to slam Norway off the puck. In their frenzy they got a little out of control. Graeme took a hooking penalty and Jean took one for elbowing.

This time Norway had a five-on-three. The puck bounced around the Canadian end. Norway knew exactly what to do — get it back to Pedersen on the point. The Norway defence waited for the perfect chance. When the puck came back to him, he moved forward and one-timed a fast shot past Rosey's glove hand. The score was 2–0. The period ended with Canada down by two goals.

Right off the start of the second period, Canada put the puck in the net. But then the ref called it back. He ruled that he had blown the whistle before the puck went over the line. Jeff argued. He sent Todd as captain over to talk to the ref. The play went to video review. Both teams waited for the final answer.

No goal!

Jeff was furious, but he told his players to shake it off. Instead, the Canadian players got angry. Todd took an interference penalty, and Norway again went on the power play. Norway cycled the puck in the Canadian zone. It didn't take long for them to put the puck past Rosey. Now they were up 3–0.

Eight minutes into the period, Mark Noot had the puck on the blue line. He looked around, taking his time. He wanted to make the perfect pass. He saw Shawn in the slot. He rifled off a pass. Shawn one-

Mark Noot (#34) and Ray Grassi (#21) crunching a player along the boards.

timed the puck and Hervé, who was right in front of the net, tipped it in. Finally, Canada was on the board.

After that, Canada had some chances. But luck wasn't with them. They just couldn't get the puck past the goalie.

Canada took three more penalties. They were successful at killing two, but on the last one Norway scored. The second period ended and Canada was losing 4–1.

In the break between periods, Jeff told the guys to settle down. He told them to play hard hockey but not take dumb penalties. They had to focus on the skilled game they knew how to play.

The Canadians listened. In the third period they did take fewer penalties and outshot Norway 6 shots to 2. But they couldn't get the puck in Johansen's net.

When the final buzzer went, the score was 4–1 for Norway.

After the loss, the players rehashed the game. They talked about what they had to do to win the gold medal.

The loss wasn't the end of the world. The team had made it to the semifinals, where they were slotted to play Germany. The players thought that Germany was an easier team to beat than the United States team that Norway had to play in the

Norway and Sledge Hockey

The Norwegian word "sledge" translates to "sled" in English. In the United States, and sometimes in Canada, the sport is called "sled hockey."

semifinals. The gold medal was still within reach.

By the time everyone was dressed and ready to get on the bus, the mood had changed. The players had gone from down to determined. They were not out yet. After the game Todd said to reporters, "Norway played a good game. We respect them both on and off the ice. If there was a game to lose, it was this one. But it doesn't mean we didn't play our best. We dominated the game in the end, but we couldn't capitalize. We didn't manage to put the puck in the net."

Back in Canada, the Hockey Canada

media relations people were busy updating the website. They posted a game summary titled, "Canada Suffers First Defeat; Advances to Play Germany in Semifinal."

The CBC in Canada wasn't so kind. Their headline read, "Norway Humbles Canada in Sledge Hockey."

9 Pressure is On

Team Germany was not to be taken lightly. Yes, Canada had beat them all year, but they were coming on strong. Germany's sledge hockey team was a Cinderella story. "The fact that we beat Germany in both of the games we played a month ago doesn't mean much," said Jean. "It's a different story now and they are playing better than before. They are at their top."

This was Canada's first big game in a

Lining up for a faceoff.

long time. The team had a bad history with big games. Could they hold on and play hard for the full game?

Both semifinal games were played on the same day. The Canadians had the late game. During the day the players rested and prepared. When the news trickled through the common room that Norway had beaten the United States in the other semifinal game, the Canadians got fired up. If they beat Germany they would have another chance to play Norway.

Before the game, the dressing room was quiet. The usual bantering and joking was missing.

Full of nervous energy, Team Canada pushed their sledges onto the ice. Rosey made some great saves in warm-up. Finally, the whistle blew to start the game.

Todd called the guys to the team huddle. If they lost, he might not have a chance to play in a gold medal game for a long time. He had to go home and get his hip better before he played in another tournament. If they lost, they weren't contenders for the gold medal.

Full of adrenalin, Canada started the game with good energy. Moments into the game, Jean took a pass in the slot and one-timed it, hitting the post. The Canadians controlled the play, but couldn't get the

Graeme Murray (#29) and Jean Labonté (#17) dumping a German player.

puck past the German goalie. At the ten-minute mark, Graeme, on defence, got the puck on the end of his stick and rushed forward. He pushed past two German players. When he got close to the net, he rifled off a shot that pinged the crossbar.

With just a little over a minute left in the first period, Jeremy rushed to the side of the net. He moved his sledge to stay open. He picked up a perfect pass and shot

Jean Labonté (#17) winning the race for the puck.

the puck. Again, the German goalie made a great save. Dany and Marc had scoring chances just seconds after Jeremy's chance, but their shots didn't turn on the red light either.

Although the Canadians had dominated the play and had outshot the Germans ten to five, they went to the dressing room with a 0–0 score. All it would take was one bad bounce and Germany could have the lead. Canada had to score, and soon.

Just one minute into the second period, Germany managed to intercept a pass. In the Canadian net, Rosey saw the two-on-one coming toward him. He kept his eyes on the puck. He had to cut his angles, limit the shooting area.

When the puck sailed over Rosey's net and not into it, cheers erupted from the Canadian bench.

Todd wanted on the ice. He had to turn this game around. At the next whistle he got his chance. He lined up for the faceoff in Germany's end. When the puck dropped, he pushed it over to Jeremy. Jeremy one-timed a slick shot. The puck sailed toward the net. It went right over the German goalie's shoulder and into the net. Todd rushed over to Jeremy and hugged him.

The goal sparked Billy and Bradley. The young guys were eager for some stats. Just three minutes later, Billy found Bradley

Bradley Bowden (#27) getting ready to make a pass.

alone and in the slot. Bradley snapped the puck. The German goalie had no chance.

With a few minutes left in the second period, Canada went to a power play. Jeff put out his young talent. Graeme sent the puck to Bradley, who gave a perfect tape pass to Billy. Billy flew down on a breakaway and picked his spot. High to the glove side, he fired off his shot.

The Canadians went to the dressing room with a 3–0 lead.

The mood in the dressing room was lighter, but the Canadians didn't want to get too confident. They wanted to finish the game right.

At 6:28 in the third period, Greg one-timed the puck and it smoked to the back of the net. Greg hugged Billy, who had sent him the pass.

Billy put in his second power-play goal of the game at 13:31. With less than a minute and a half to play, the Canadians knew they had won. Still, they kept up the pace. Those on the bench watched the clock tick, the time melt away. Most of the players couldn't wait to hear the buzzer.

When the buzzer finally sounded, the team sped over to Rosey. Before lining up to shake hands with the German players, they huddled together, hugging each other. They had won 5–0 in the semifinal. They were going on to play in the gold medal game.

This time, back in Canada, the CBC had good news to report. The headlines read, "Canada to Play for Sledge Hockey Gold."

On the morning of the gold-medal game in Turin, Shawn woke up from a dream. In it, his team had won 3–0.

Excitement after winning a big game.

Rosey also woke up with a dream in his head. He had dreamed that the Canadians had won 3–0. The score in his dream made him a bit nervous. Why did he have to dream about getting a shutout?

At breakfast, Shawn sat down beside Rosey. Rosey mumbled his hello to Shawn. As they ate, Shawn told Rosey about his dream. Amazed, Rosey told Shawn he had had the same dream.

That afternoon Jeff wanted everyone to meet for a video session and team meeting. He had something to pass on to the players. NHL and Olympic coach Pat Quinn had called and told Jeff to wish the players good luck. A coaching icon, Quinn had said he would be cheering for them back in Canada.

Jeff also wanted the team to watch a DVD recording of the game they had played against Norway. He wanted them to see their mistakes and talk about what they could do better.

As the players watched the video, they talked throughout. The mood was definitely positive.

Everyone looked at their own mistakes, but also at the good things they had done. No one blamed anyone for the loss against Norway. No one pointed a finger at the players who had taken the penalties. No one argued. Everyone talked about how they could improve. They talked about the changes they needed to make for the game that was to take place later that night.

In the middle of the discussion, there was a knock on the door. Puzzled, Jeff put the DVD player on pause.

Scott cracked open the door. "Sorry to interrupt, Jeff. But I've got a phone call for you guys," he said. Scott put his cell phone on the table. "Wayne Gretzky wants to say something." He spoke into his phone. "Wayne, you there?"

"I'm here," said a familiar voice.

"Go ahead, they're listening," said Scott.

"I just wanted to wish you guys good luck," they heard Wayne say through the speaker phone. "Since the Men's Olympic team didn't get the job done, we're counting on you guys to bring home the gold."

Wayne Gretzky was Canada's hockey hero. Had he really taken time out of his busy life to wish them good luck? The sledge hockey players all left the room that afternoon feeling proud and honoured to be part of Team Canada. The nerves had turned to positive energy.

When the announcement came that the ice was ready, both teams filed out of their dressing rooms. Ray got on his skateboard and pushed his way to the ice. When he got to the ramp, the Italian arena staff were waiting for him. They gave him a thumbs-up. Then they pushed him up the ramp.

As soon as the Canadians flew onto the ice, the crowd yelled, "Go, Canada, Go!" Canadian flags waved.

Todd enjoyed the moment he had waited so long for. He shoved his pick in the ice and pushed his sledge beside Shawn and Hervé, the other veterans on the team.

Shawn said later that he felt a huge weight on his shoulders. He knew that Canadian fans back home were cheering for them. With each game they played, more fans and more media paid attention. For the gold-medal game there would be five or six video cameras and between 15 and 20 still cameras recording their play. Reporters from CBC, Radio-Canada, Canadian Press, and the *Vancouver Sun* were there. Even Wayne Gretzky was cheering for them. If they didn't win, Shawn felt he would be letting down all those people.

Rosey cruised to his net and turned to face his players. With confidence, he warmed up.

After the warm-up, Jeff pulled the guys together for their last pre-game huddle in the 2006 Paralympic Games.

10 The Final Game

As soon as the ref dropped the puck for the opening faceoff, the shoving started. Nerves flared. Both teams took to the attack. Although Canada tried to get down the ice, Norway's defence kept stopping them.

Two minutes into the game, Canada didn't have one shot on net. The Norwegian defender had the puck. Billy shoved his pick into the ice and flew toward him. He wanted that puck. Billy used every ounce of strength he had to fore-check. He battled with the Norwegian defence against the boards until he had the puck on his stick.

Billy circled around the back of the net. He glanced up to check who was open. Bradley tapped his stick on the ice. Billy passed the puck and Bradley rifled the puck on a one-timer. The puck sailed into the back of the net.

It was the first shot on net for Canada, and it went in!

The fans went crazy. At 2:52 into the game, Canada had an early lead.

They played hard hockey, but the Canadians couldn't put the puck in the net again in the first period. But neither could Norway. Canada stayed controlled and took just one penalty. At the end of the first, the score was 1–0 for Canada.

The Canadians knew there was a lot of game left. One mistake and the game could change. In the dressing room they talked strategy. They needed to play good, defensive hockey.

The Canadians followed their plan perfectly, holding off Norway. In the middle of the second period, Norway had only one shot on net. They started getting riled. They elbowed and pushed and grabbed jerseys. The Canadians kept their cool, knowing they could draw some

Past Team Canada Paralympic Results

- 1994 in Lillehammer, Norway:
  Gold – Sweden; Silver – Norway; Bronze – Canada
- 1998 in Nagano, Japan:
  Gold – Norway; Silver – Canada; Bronze – Sweden
- 2002 in Salt Lake City, USA:
  Gold – USA; Silver – Norway; Bronze – Sweden

penalties. Norway's first penalty of the period was for holding. But Canada just couldn't make good on the one-man advantage. The second Norway penalty was four minutes later for elbowing.

On the power play, Canada moved the puck around, back and forth, up and down. Then Bradley saw an opening. In a risky move, he zipped past Norway's defender. Instead of shooting on the net, he made a drop pass to Greg. Greg zinged off a high wrist shot. The puck flew over the goalie's shoulder and the red light shone.

When the buzzer sounded ending the second period 30 seconds later, Canada went to the dressing room with a 2–0 lead.

Rosey said later that he didn't want to think of his dream of winning, of getting a shutout. There was still a period left to play. He didn't want to jinx their game. Shawn might have been thinking about his dream too, but he didn't say anything to Rosey.

As soon as the puck dropped to start the third period, Norway hustled. They were not giving up yet. They stormed past the Canadians every chance they got.

The time ticked. Rosey kept focused. He stopped shot after shot. Sometimes, he didn't even know how he had made the saves. He just made them.

With one minute left to play, Norway pulled their goalie. This gave them another attacker. The play was in Canada's end. Norway passed the puck around, looking for an opening to score.

Billy moved his sledge, trying to force Norway to make a bad pass. He batted and batted, trying to get the puck on his stick. Like a ping pong ball, the puck went from defence to defence. Norway wasn't giving up the puck. Billy pushed forward. He touched the puck. Then he had it on the end of his stick. He drilled the puck down the ice toward the empty net. When the puck cruised over the goal line, the Canadian fans went crazy. Billy started to cry. With eight seconds left in the game, he had scored.

Both Shawn and Rosey looked up at the scoreboard. Talk about dreams coming true. Were they really going to win this game 3–0?

From the bench, Jeff yelled for Shawn, Todd, and Hervé to take the final faceoff.

The three veterans dug in their picks and pushed their sledges to centre ice. Todd had tears streaming down his face. Shawn says that at that moment, he felt the heavy weight lift from his shoulders. It was a bunch of things combined: relief, pride, glory. Hervé grinned at his teammates. Jeff had made sure that the three veterans would be bringing home the game. The puck dropped, the clock ticked, and the buzzer sounded.

Canada's sledge hockey team had won the gold medal!

Jean Labonté (#17) and Billy Bridges (#18) hug after winning.

11 O Canada!

The players from both teams lined up on their blue lines. The Canadian players

Players lined up after winning the gold medal. From left to right - Paul Rosen, Hervé Lord, Marc Dorion, Bradley Bowden, Shawn Matheson, Dany Verner,

clapped as each Norway player received a silver medal. Then the announcement was made. Canada had won the 2006 Sledge Hockey Paralympic gold medal.

One by one, the Canadian players lowered their heads so the medals could be draped around their necks. They shook hands with the dignitaries for the Paralympic Games.

After receiving gold medals and yellow roses, the Canadian sledge players lined up to sing "O Canada." Throughout the arena, the music for the Canadian anthem

Benoit St-Amand, Jeremy Booker, Mark Noot, Graeme Murray, Ray Grassi, Greg Westlake, Billy Bridges, Jean Labonté, Todd Nicholson.

played. The players, both veterans and rookies, sang with great gusto as the Canadian flag was lowered from the ceiling. All around them, cameras snapped their picture, and video cameras shot footage of their victory. Fans sang along with the players. But the players sang the loudest. In their minds they relived the journey, trying to hold this final moment for as long as they could.

All the players on Team Canada had played their hearts out. They had played for their families, who had sacrificed a lot to get the team there. They had played for each other. And they were bringing gold home to Canada.

After the ice ceremony the guys sailed around the ice, wearing their medals and waving their yellow roses. They granted the media their interviews. Coach Jeff was the first in line to talk to reporters. "I'm really excited for my players," he said.

"We've worked extremely hard for the past four years. We were really disciplined tonight and really focused on doing the job."

"I'm feeling absolutely wonderful," said Big Ray Grassi. "Couldn't be better. We played an awesome game tonight and did exactly what we wanted to do. We were able to control the game."

When the microphone was put in front of Jeremy Booker, he said, "I think it was just adrenalin, the rush of the crowd. That definitely gets me going and I think our fans had a negative effect on Norway."

"It is quite the honour," said team captain Todd Nicholson. "I didn't do it by myself, there were fifteen guys out there and we all played our part. After everything I have been through in the past year, it makes it all worthwhile."

Of course, Greg Westlake couldn't wait to get in a few words to the CBC. "I'm a hockey nut. I saw the juniors go on their long (gold medal run) and sing *O Canada*, saw World Championships, Olympics. It was my time to do the same, so I wasn't going to let it go to waste. I brutally murdered the anthem but it was a fun time doing it."

After all the interviews and excitement the players headed off the ice. In the dressing room, they kept telling jokes and

We're number one. From left to right - Graeme Murray, Ray Grassi, Greg Westlake, Billy Bridges and Jean Labonté.

talking about the game. Then the Italian team and Big Ray's arena friends came down to celebrate with the Canadians.

They laughed and talked for hours. The arena staff kept coming by, telling them they had to leave. But they didn't want to leave. They wanted to make the moment last forever.

Epilogue

Since the 2006 Paralympics in Turin, the Canadian sledge hockey team has come on strong. Sledge hockey is becoming more known by all kinds of people. *Sledhead*, a documentary about the team, has let more and more people know about the sport. Sledge hockey is fast growing as a spectator sport.

The Canadian team has continued to play some big games against Norway. In the 2007 World Sledge Hockey Challenge in Kelowna, BC, Canada beat Norway in the final game. The score was 0–0 at the end of the third period. Just 48 seconds into the sudden-death overtime period, Bradley Bowden scored. The Canadian crowd loved the win.

Then in the 2008 World Championship in Marlborough, Massachusetts, in the United States, Canada once again went

Sledge Hockey for kids

- In 2007, the City of Toronto and Bloorview Kids Rehab started a sledge hockey program that is open to all ages and abilities. (They even had an exhibition game at Toronto's City hall with some of the 2006 Paralympic players.)
- Easter Seals in Newfoundland and Labrador also brings sledge hockey to kids with physical disabilities. Easter Seals wants to make sure that hockey is not just limited to able-bodied players.
- In the spring of 2004, Hockey Alberta decided to include sledge hockey in its programs for the following year. The sport is played in Edmonton and Calgary and is open to all ages.

head-to-head with Norway in the final game. This time the score was 2–2 with nine seconds left in the game when Greg Westlake scored. It was a thrilling finish to another Canadian gold medal. Adam

Dixon, who didn't play in 2006, and Billy Bridges scored the other two goals. In both of those tournaments, the United States picked up the bronze medal.

Late in November 2008, the Canadian Sledge Team headed to Charlottetown, PEI, for the 2008 World Sledge Hockey Challenge. Again Canada met up with Norway. Marc Dorion and Greg Westlake each got two goals to lead their team to a 7–0 victory before a large crowd at the CARI complex. Members of the sledge team took time during the tournament to invite children and adults to try out their sledges. Many keen PEI fans sat in sledges that were provided by Hockey Canada.

The 2009 National Sledge Team was announced in early February of that year. They competed in the Hockey Canada Cup from February 24 to March 1 in Vancouver. The 17-player roster included 15 players from the gold–winning 2008

IPC Sledge Hockey World Championship Team, and 14 players who competed in the 2006 Paralympic Games. Teams from Germany, Japan, and the United States participated. The final game, televised on TSN and played in front of 1,812 fans, ended in a dramatic shootout. Adam Dixon scored the only shootout goal to give Canada a 2–1 victory and the gold medal.

As head coach for Team Canada at the 2010 Paralympic Games in Vancouver, BC, Jeff Snyder said again that the win in Turin, Italy, in 2006 raised sledge hockey awareness across Canada.

"There is tipping, there are slapshots, there are one timers. Body checks, wrist shots, penalty shots; there are battles in the crease." explained Billy Bridges, talking about sledge hockey at the 2010 Paralympics "When people see that it is like hockey, then we can keep fans, that's for sure."

Glossary

Able-bodied: A person who is able-bodied has a body that is physically strong and healthy.

Amputation: When arms or legs are removed, by accident or by surgery.

Amputee: A person who has had an arm or a leg removed.

Checking: Physically keeping another player in check.

Defence: On each team there is one goalie, three forwards, and two defence. The job of the defence is to keep the puck away from the goalie.

Demonstration sport: A sport played to promote itself on the international level. In the Olympics and Paralympics, medals are awarded for these events, but medals are not included in a team's medal tally.

Disabled: In sledge hockey, the players must have a lower body disability to play. This means that they have an impairment in the lower body that makes ordinary skating — and playing hockey — impossible.

Faceoff: When the play starts there is a faceoff. All the players line up and a centre from each team lines up at the circle. When the referee drops the puck, the two centres try to get the puck and pass it to one of their teammates.

Final game: The game that takes place between the two top teams in a tournament.

Fore-check: When a team is trying to get a goal and they are in the other team's end zone, they can rush forward and try to take the puck from the defence. This is called fore-checking.

Forward: A player who is part of the forward line of the offence.

Man advantage: When one team gets to play with one more player than the other team. This happens when one team gets a penalty.

Overtime: If a game is tied at the end of three periods, the game will go into overtime. In sledge hockey, the overtime period is fifteen minutes long.

Paralympic Games: An elite sporting event for athletes from six different disability groups.

Paraplegia: Impairment in function of the lower body. Paraplegia usually affects both legs.

Paraplegic: A person who has paraplegia.

Penalty: When a player does something that is against the rules of the sport, a penalty is called.

Penalty kill: The player that commits a penalty must go to the penalty box. This leaves the player's team with only four skaters on the ice. Because the team has to play with one man short they have to do what is called a penalty kill — they have to work hard to play during the time that their player is in the penalty box because they have one less player.

Power play: When the opposing team takes a penalty, the team without the penalty goes to what is called a power play. They get to play for the length of the penalty with a man advantage. Many goals are scored on the power play.

Prosthetic: An artificial extension that replaces a body part.

Semi-final: A game that takes place before the final game of a tournament. This game determines who will play in the gold medal game and who will play in the bronze medal game.

Shootout: When a game is finished and an overtime period has been played, sometimes there is a shootout.

Each team picks three players to shoot on the goalie. The player lines up at centre ice, skates toward the goalie, and tries to get a goal. The competition is only between the player and the goalie.

Shutout: When a goalie doesn't allow any goals for an entire game.

Spina bifida: A birth defect in which the spinal cord is not completely formed.

Stick-handling: When a player skates down the ice with the puck on the end of his stick. He moves the puck back and forth as he skates. This is called stick-handling.

Veteran: A person who has had a lot of experience in an activity.

Acknowledgements

Recording history requires help from so many people. I have to thank first and foremost the athletes and Jeff Snyder for responding to my e-mails and phone calls. Adam Crockett at the Hockey Canada office was invaluable to me and even went so far as to proofread my manuscript. I would like to also thank all of the other HC staff members for providing me with information, photos and precious memories. And of course, a book is never complete without an editorial staff. Thanks to everyone at James Lorimer & Company for their guidance.

About the Author

Lorna Schultz Nicholson is a full-time writer in Calgary, where she lives with her husband, Hockey Canada President Bob Nicholson, and their three children. She is the author of a fiction hockey series in the Lorimer Sports Stories, including *Too Many Men* which was nominated for the Diamond Willow award. This is her second book in the Recordbooks series. Her first was titled *Pink Power*.

Photo Credits

Thanks to Hockey Canada for providing all of the photos, including front and back cover, for this book.

Index